⭐ Contents

This powerful forklift is lifting a heavy object off a truck.

⊛ What is a forklift?

A forklift is a machine made for lifting heavy loads. It helps people stack things into piles. It helps people place things on shelves. It helps people load and unload trucks, ships, and airplanes.

⭐ What are the parts of a forklift?

A forklift has two strong, metal bars called **forks**. The forks slide under items to be lifted. Often the items are on a flat **pallet**. Putting things on pallets makes them easier to stack. The forklift's forks slip right into the pallet.

pallet

forks

The main photo shows the forks on a forklift.
The small photo shows a forklift lifting a pallet.

This worker is lifting flattened boxes high overhead.

mast

★ The forks move up and down on the **mast**. The mast is on the front of the forklift. It is taller than the forklift's body. It can raise the forks high overhead.

★ A forklift's **carriage** is a flat metal plate. It keeps the load from slipping backward. The forklift's driver can tip the mast, too. This keeps the load from falling off.

carriage

You can see this forklift's carriage and forks.

This operator is using the steering wheel to turn.

⭐ Who drives a forklift?

A forklift's driver is called the **operator**. The operator sits in the **cab**. The cab has lots of **controls**. Some controls lift, lower, or tip the load. Others move the forklift forward and backward. A steering wheel turns the forklift.

★ Are there different kinds of forklifts?

Forklifts come in many shapes and sizes. Smaller ones can lift smaller loads. Bigger ones can lift heavier loads. Some forklifts have different kinds of lifting parts. They are used for different jobs.

14

This huge forklift is moving giant tires.

This forklift is moving heavy loads from ships onto trucks.

⭐ How are forklifts used?

Forklifts are used for many lifting jobs. They are often used in shipyards and airports. Ships and airplanes carry lots of items from place to place. Forklifts help people load and unload these items.

★ **Warehouses** are buildings where items are stored. Warehouse workers use forklifts to stack the items. They use forklifts to set the items on shelves. They also use forklifts to load and unload trucks.

This worker is using a forklift to pull items from a high shelf.

This worker is stacking items on a warehouse shelf. ⭐

⊛ Are forklifts important?

Forklifts work all around us. Many things are too heavy for people to lift. But forklifts can lift them easily. They help people stack the items into neat, tidy piles. Forklifts are very important!

21

⊛ Glossary

cab (KAB) A machine's cab is the area where the driver sits.

carriage (KAYR-ij) A forklift's carriage is a flat plate that keeps loads from tipping backward.

controls (kun-TROLZ) Controls are parts that people use to run a machine.

forks (FORKS) A forklift's forks are strong metal arms.

mast (MAST) A forklift's mast is the part that lifts the forks.

operator (AH-pur-ay-tur) A machine's operator is the person who runs the machine.

pallet (PAL-let) A pallet is a flat wooden or plastic square used for stacking things.

warehouses (WAYR-how-sez) Warehouses are buildings where items are stored until people need them.

 Books

Barkan, Joanne. *Big Wheels.* Mahwah, NJ: Whistlestop/Troll, 1996.

Simon, Seymour. *Seymour Simon's Book of Trucks.* New York: HarperCollins Publishers, 2000.

Zuehlke, Jeffrey. *Forklifts.* Minneapolis, MN: Lerner Publications, 2007.

 Web Sites

Visit our Web page for lots of links about forklifts:
http://www.childsworld.com/links

Note to parents, teachers, and librarians: We routinely check our Web links to make sure they're safe, active sites—so encourage your readers to check them out!

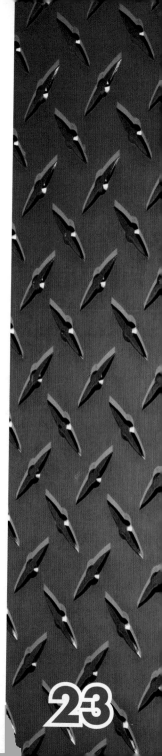

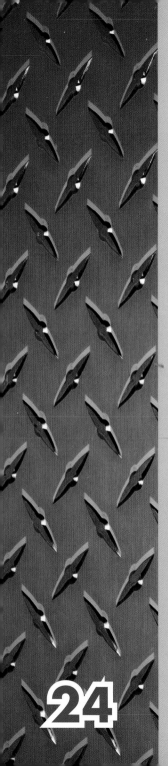

★ Index

★ About the Author

Marv Alinas has lived in Minnesota for over thirty years. When she's not reading or writing, Marv enjoys spending time with her dog and traveling to small river towns in northeastern Iowa and western Wisconsin.